To God Be

the

Glory

© 2013 by Barbour Publishing, Inc.

Written and compiled by Gale Hyatt.

ISBN 978-1-62416-628-0

Adobe Digital Edition (.epub) 978-1-62836-287-9
Kindle and MobiPocket Edition (.prc) 978-1-62836-288-6

All rights reserved. No part of this publication may be reproduced or transmitted for commercial purposes, except for brief quotations in printed reviews, without written permission of the publisher.

Scripture quotations marked KJV are taken from the King James Version of the Bible.

Scripture quotations marked NIV are taken from the HOLY BIBLE, NEW INTERNATIONAL VERSION®. NIV®. Copyright © 1973, 1978, 1984, 2011 by Biblica, Inc.™ Used by permission. All rights reserved worldwide.

Scripture quotations marked NLT are taken from the Holy Bible. New Living Translation copyright© 1996, 2004, 2007 by Tyndale House Foundation. Used by permission of Tyndale House Publishers, Inc. Carol Stream, Illinois 60188. All rights reserved.

Scripture quotations marked ESV are from The Holy Bible, English Standard Version®, copyright © 2001 by Crossway Bibles, a publishing ministry of Good News Publishers. Used by permission. All rights reserved.

Published by Barbour Publishing, Inc., P.O. Box 719, Uhrichsville, Ohio 44683, www.barbourbooks.com

Our mission is to publish and distribute inspirational products offering exceptional value and biblical encouragement to the masses.

Member of the
Evangelical Christian
Publishers Association

Printed in the United States of America.

To God Be the

the

Glory

Inspiration from the Beloved Hymn

BARBOUR
PUBLISHING

Contents

To God Be the Glory. 6

Great Things He Has Done 9

Amazing Love 21

Yielding 33

The Life Gate 45

Perfect Redemption. 57

The Purchase of Blood 69

Mercy's Pardon 81

Promises. 93

True Belief 105

Gathering Wisdom 117

His Still, Small Voice. 129

Rejoicing in Jesus. 141

Gathering for Praise. 153

Cast Your Crown 165

Glorious 177

To God Be the Glory

To God be the glory,
great things He has done;
So loved He the world that
He gave us His Son,
Who yielded His life an
atonement for sin,
And opened the life gate that all may go in.

Refrain
Praise the Lord, praise the Lord,
Let the earth hear His voice!
Praise the Lord, praise the Lord,
Let the people rejoice!
O come to the Father,
through Jesus the Son,
And give Him the glory,
great things He has done.

O perfect redemption,
the purchase of blood,
To every believer the promise of God;
The vilest offender who truly believes,
That moment from Jesus a pardon receives.

Great things He has taught us,
great things He has done,
And great our rejoicing
through Jesus the Son;
But purer, and higher, and greater will be
Our wonder, our transport,
when Jesus we see.

Lyrics by Fanny Crosby, 1875

Great Things
He Has Done

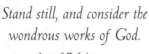

*Stand still, and consider the
wondrous works of God.*

JOB 37:14 KJV

There are plenty of things in this life to worry
about. We face difficult decisions with life-
long consequences. There are health issues and
finances to fret over, family responsibilities to
juggle, and hectic schedules to meet. Our prayer
lists overflow. With so much demanding our
attention, it's easy to become discouraged. But
however mountainous our problems appear, God
is bigger. His blessings to us are innumerable. All
we have to do is remember them.

Gaze up at the night sky, alight with moon
and stars. Behold the intricate network of veins
in a simple leaf. All of nature—from the tallest
mountain to the tiniest living organism—was
brought into existence by the great Creator's *"let
there be. . . ."*

He who placed the sun and commanded it to shine by day also parted the seas for His people and fed them with bread from heaven. By His power, a virgin gave birth to a Son. By His will, that Son died on a cross to restore mankind's lost innocence. His loving arms are stretched wide to receive the broken-hearted, and His kiss of forgiveness removes our shameful guilt.

Truly the Lord is good! His mercies are new every morning. He showers us with good things and abundantly supplies our every need. No matter how difficult the journey becomes, let us never forget the works of Almighty God. Instead, let us cry with the psalmist: "Great is the Lord, and greatly to be praised." (Psalm 48:1)

Among the gods there is none like you, Lord; no deeds can compare with yours. . . . For you are great and do marvelous deeds; you alone are God.

PSALM 86:8, 10 NIV

*God's voice thunders in marvelous ways;
he does great things beyond our understanding.*

JOB 37:5 NIV

*It is he who made the earth by his power,
who established the world by his wisdom,
and by his understanding stretched out the heavens.*

JEREMIAH 10:12 ESV

Were there no God, we would be
in this glorious world with grateful
hearts and no one to thank.

CHRISTINA ROSSETTI

There is no creature so poor or so low that
he may not look up with childish confidence
and say, "My Father, Thou art mine."

HENRY WARD BEECHER

This is my Father's world: why should my heart
be sad? The Lord is King; let the heavens ring!
God reigns; let the earth be glad!

MALTBIE DAVENPORT BABCOCK

Only fear the LORD, and serve him in truth with all your heart: for consider how great things he hath done for you.

I SAMUEL 12:24 KJV

You have given me the shield of your salvation, and your right hand supported me, and your gentleness made me great.

PSALM 18:35 ESV

Debt of Gratitude

Almighty Father, You are Lord of creation and
Lord of my life. You have blessed me in more
ways than I could ever recount. You give me
the strength to press on despite my trials.
Your courage enables me to do things that I
thought were impossible. I can never repay Your
goodness, dear Lord, but I can praise You.
And with my whole heart, I do so. *Amen.*

When I consider your heavens, the work of your fingers,
the moon and the stars, which you have set in place,
what is mankind that you are mindful of them,
human beings that you care for them?

PSALM 8:3–4 NIV

And God said, Let there be light:
and there was light.

GENESIS 1:3 KJV

The heavens proclaim the glory of God. The skies display
his craftsmanship. Day after day they continue to speak;
night after night they make him known.

PSALM 19:1–2 NLT

Nature is a looking-glass in which
I see the face of God.

CHARLES H. SPURGEON

I love to think of nature as an unlimited
broadcasting station, through which
God speaks to us every hour,
if we will only tune in.

GEORGE WASHINGTON CARVER

For by him were all things created, that are in heaven, and that are in earth, visible and invisible, whether they be thrones, or dominions, or principalities, or powers: all things were created by him, and for him.

COLOSSIANS 1:16 KJV

He telleth the number of the stars; he calleth them all by their names. Great is our Lord, and of great power: his understanding is infinite.

PSALM 147:4–5 KJV

Praise from the Heart

Dear heavenly Father, words cannot express my gratitude for all You have done for me. You love me in spite of my failures and shortcomings. You come to my rescue when I call. When I am weak and hurting, Your love comforts me. Though my requests are many, they are never too much for You to handle. For all that You are and continue to be, I thank You. *Amen.*

You can tell the size of your God by looking at the size of your worry list. The longer your list, the smaller your God.

UNKNOWN

There are three stages in the work of God: impossible, difficult, done.

JAMES HUDSON TAYLOR

Don't forget to pray today because God didn't forget to wake you up this morning.

UNKNOWN

Amazing Love

For God so loved the world, that he gave his only begotten Son, that whosoever believeth in Him should not perish, but have everlasting life.

JOHN 3:16 KJV

Do we ever doubt God's love for us? We wouldn't be human if we didn't. Sometimes we pass through seasons of discouragement when it feels like nobody understands or cares. Such is the problem with feelings. Sky high today, plunging tomorrow.

God's Word reminds us that, no matter how we feel, nothing can separate us from His love. If we're uncertain of this, we have only to look at Calvary. Nothing but the fiercest, most sincere love could keep Jesus on the cross when it was in His power to call for rescue. His passion for our eternal souls demanded that He give Himself for our sins, not only to grant us everlasting life but also to make us joyful in this one.

God delights in our happiness. Such is the nature of His love. Unlike our human passions that burn with molten fervor in one season, then grow frigid with frost in the next, God's love is forever constant. Forged in the dawning of time, tested throughout the ages, written in stone and sealed with blood, it is ours eternally.

Remember that in your times of loneliness, when friends are distant and family ties unravel, when hardships strike and griefs assail. The God who did not spare His only Son for your sake will never leave you. His love endures forever.

But God showed his great love for us by sending Christ to die for us while we were still sinners.

ROMANS 5:8 NLT

This is real love—not that we loved God, but that he loved us and sent his Son as a sacrifice to take away our sins.

1 JOHN 4:10 NLT

Who shall separate us from the love of Christ?

ROMANS 8:35 KJV

God loves each of us as if there
were only one of us.

SAINT AUGUSTINE

Who, being loved, is poor?

OSCAR WILDE

Christ did not die that God might love us,
but He died because God loved us.

CHARLES HODGE

*He brought me to the banqueting house,
and his banner over me was love.*

SONG OF SOLOMON 2:4 KJV

*All glory to him who loves us and
has freed us from our sins by
shedding his blood for us.*

REVELATION 1:5 NLT

*See what kind of love the Father
has given to us, that we should be
called children of God.*

I JOHN 3:1 ESV

Love's Sacrifice

Dear Father, You have proven Your love to me over and over again. And yet, I so often need Your reassurance. In my dark times, when I am fretful and weak, lead me to the cross. Remind me that it was there that You showed your unconditional love to me. You gave all to redeem my life from destruction. Now, help me to walk worthy of that great sacrifice. *Amen.*

The beloved of the LORD dwells in safety. The High God surrounds him all day long, and dwells between his shoulders.

DEUTERONOMY 33:12 ESV

Live a life filled with love, following the example of Christ. He loved us and offered himself as a sacrifice for us, a pleasing aroma to God.

EPHESIANS 5:2 NLT

He that spared not his own Son, but delivered him up for us all, how shall he not with him also freely give us all things?

ROMANS 8:32 KJV

There is no surprise more magical than
the surprise of being loved: It is
God's finger on man's shoulder.

CHARLES MORGAN

To say that I am made in the image of
God is to say that love is the reason
for my existence, for God is love.

THOMAS À KEMPIS

The greatest honor we can give Almighty
God is to live gladly because of the
knowledge of his love.

JULIAN OF NORWICH

*For I am persuaded, that neither death,
nor life, nor angels, nor principalities,
nor powers, nor things present, nor
things to come, nor height, nor depth,
nor any other creature, shall be able to
separate us from the love of God, which
is in Christ Jesus our Lord.*

ROMANS 8:38–39 KJV

Love never fails.

I CORINTHIANS 13:8 NIV

Assuring Love

Dear Lord, sometimes I feel so lonely and unloved. I crave Your sweet assurance. It strengthens me in ways that I could never describe. Speak comfort to my heart when I am sad. Remind me that, no matter how I feel, You are with me always. Draw me closer and closer until my love toward You is as fervent as Yours is for me. *Amen.*

My Jesus I love thee, I know thou art mine,
For thee all thy follies of sin I resign;
My gracious Redeemer, my Savior art thou;
If ever I loved thee, my Jesus 'tis now.

WILLIAM FEATHERSTONE

Love is the beauty of the soul.

ST. AUGUSTINE

Yielding

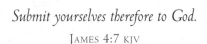

Submit yourselves therefore to God.

JAMES 4:7 KJV

𝒩othing brings more relief than surrendering our will to God and allowing Him to mold us into the woman He wants us to be. But doing so sounds much easier than it is. We have an enemy, and her name is Self.

Self demands to have her own way. She resists the authority of her husband, scorning the notion that God expects her to submit to a man. She sees a friend's counsel as interference. Parental advice seems meddlesome. The boss isn't fair, and the government is corrupt. She is attracted to others just like her, although she secretly detests them. When she is in control, our lives are miserable. Only by surrendering to God can we defeat her.

When we have yielded to our Savior, we delight in obeying Him. Though Self rises at every opportunity to reclaim her throne, we resist her, preferring the blessings of God to her spiteful charms. We recognize that submission to husbands, pastors, parents, workplace authority, and government (though it may indeed be corrupt!) is really submission to God.

If Self seems hard to defeat, we should journey to Calvary. There, we find the very portrait of submission. Though divine, Christ was still human. He didn't want to suffer and die. But He kept His self consecrated to His Father's will, knowing that doing so would earn the greatest triumph in the end.

And it did. We are the bounty of His submission.

Father, if thou be willing, remove this cup from me:
nevertheless not my will, but thine, be done.

LUKE 22:42 KJV

Humble yourselves, therefore, under the mighty hand of
God so that at the proper time he may exalt you.

I PETER 5:6 ESV

Neither go back in fear and misgiving to the past, nor in anxiety and forecasting to the future, but lie quiet under His hand, having no will but His.

H. E. MANNING

Perfect submission, all is at rest,
I in my Savior am happy and blest;
Watching and waiting, looking above,
Filled with his goodness, lost in his love.

FANNY J. CROSBY

No soul can be really at rest until it has given up all dependence on everything else and has been forced to depend on the Lord alone.

HANNAH WHITALL SMITH

Wives, submit to your own husbands, as to the Lord.

EPHESIANS 5:22 ESV

Obey your leaders and submit to them, for they are keeping watch over your souls, as those who will have to give an account. Let them do this with joy and not with groaning, for that would be of no advantage to you.

HEBREWS 13:17 ESV

Submit yourselves for the Lord's sake to every human authority.

1 PETER 2:13 NIV

Yielding to God

Dear God, although I know that you have my best interest at heart, it's not always easy to submit to Your will. Sometimes You lead me to places that I don't want to go and ask me to do things that I don't want to do. When I find myself resisting Your will, remind me of the sacrifice that Jesus made, and help me to be as selfless as He was. *Amen.*

Be ye therefore followers
of God, as dear children. . . .

EPHESIANS 5:1 KJV

Trust in the LORD with all your heart and lean not on
your own understanding; in all your ways submit to
him, and he will make your paths straight.

PROVERBS 3:5–6 NIV

Let this be thy whole endeavour, this thy prayer, this thy desire—that thou mayest be stripped of all selfishness, and with entire simplicity follow Jesus only.

THOMAS À KEMPIS

The soul that waits upon the Lord is the soul that is entirely surrendered to Him, and that trusts Him perfectly.

HANNAH WHITALL SMITH

I have held many things in my hands, and I have lost them all; but whatever I have placed in God's hands, that I still possess.

MARTIN LUTHER

Submit to God, and you will have peace;
then things will go well for you.

JOB 22:21 NLT

What is more pleasing to the LORD:
your burnt offerings and sacrifices
or your obedience to his voice?
Listen! Obedience is better than
sacrifice, and submission is better
than offering the fat of rams.

I SAMUEL 15:22 NLT

Yielding to Others

Lord, I know that the only way to be truly happy is to obey Your Word. The scriptures tell me to submit to my husband, honor my parents, and obey those who are responsible for me. Sometimes I have a hard time doing that. Remind me that when I yield to others, I am really yielding to You. Help me to rule over Self instead of letting Self rule me. *Amen.*

We might well pray for God to invade
and conquer us, for until He does,
we remain in peril from a thousand foes.

A. W. Tozer

Be God or let God.

Unknown

I have yielded myself to thy service
And thy presence my bosom doth fill;
O my Savior, I haste to obey thee
And my heart says amen to thy will.

Charles W. Naylor

The Life Gate

*And it shall come to pass, that whosoever shall
call on the name of the Lord shall be saved.*

ACTS 2:21 KJV

*R*egardless of race. Regardless of education.
Regardless of financial status or family
ancestry, anyone can have a relationship with
Almighty God. The life gate was thrown wide
open at Calvary, when Jesus declared with His
final breaths, "It is finished." At that moment,
the curtain blocking the entrance into the Most
Holy Place where God dwelt was torn in half.
He who had been known only to the Jewish
nation and their proselytes became available to
whosoever.

Rather than conquering Rome and
reestablishing Israel's kingdom as His kinsman
hoped, Jesus set up a spiritual one, one so
mighty that even the powers of Hell can never
destroy it. He welcomes His subjects from all

walks of life, having paved the way for every man, woman, and child to enter. There's no need to prove lineages or perform painful rites. The costly entrance fee, far too high for anyone's purse, has already been paid. All the Lord requires is a heart willing to serve Him.

Have you passed through the life gate? Jesus bids everyone who is weary and thirsty to come. Shed your burdens; drink freely from the water of life. Let Him take your filthy rags and clothe you in the white robe of righteousness. His city is glorious, and He eagerly waits to welcome you inside.

I am the way, the truth, and the life. No one can come to the Father except through me.

JOHN 14:6 NLT

Behold, I stand at the door, and knock: if any man hear my voice, and open the door, I will come in to him, and will sup with him, and he with me.

REVELATION 3:20 KJV

There is peace and joy in the Lord today,
more than all in this world of sin;
There's a happy life in the holy way,
Praise the Lord, I have entered in!

BARNEY E. WARREN

Whosoever cometh, need not delay
Now the door is open, enter while you may;
Jesus is the true, the only Living Way:
Whosoever will may come.

PHILIP P. BLISS

And the Spirit and the bride say,
Come. And let him that heareth say,
Come. And let him that is athirst come.
And whosoever will, let him take
the water of life freely.

REVELATION 22:17 KJV

For by grace are ye saved through
faith; and that not of yourselves:
it is the gift of God: Not of works,
lest any man should boast.

EPHESIANS 2:8–9 KJV

Lord, to whom shall we go?
thou hast the words of eternal life.

JOHN 6:68 KJV

A Grateful Heart

Lord, when I cried out for help, You heard me. I had nothing to offer but my broken heart and wasted life, but You took me in anyway. Thank You for holding the gate open for me and for casting my sins into the Sea of Forgetfulness. I am grateful to be Your child. Teach me Your will, and use my life in whatever way You see fit. *Amen.*

For I am not ashamed of the gospel of Christ:
for it is the power of God unto salvation to every one
that believeth; to the Jew first, and also to the Greek.

ROMANS 1:16 KJV

Because of his grace he declared us righteous and
gave us confidence that we will inherit eternal life.

TITUS 3:7 NLT

I am happy today and the sun shines bright,
The clouds have been rolled away;
For the Savior said "Whosoever will"
May come with Him to stay.

J. EDWIN MCCONNELL

No man can resolve
himself into Heaven.

DWIGHT L. MOODY

*Whoever believes in the
Son has eternal life.*

JOHN 3:36 NIV

*I have been sent to proclaim faith to
those God has chosen and to teach them
to know the truth that shows them how
to live godly lives. This truth gives them
confidence that they have eternal life,
which God—who does not lie—
promised them before the world began.*

TITUS 1:1–2 NLT

Chosen

Dear Father, who am I that You would allow me to enter Your glorious kingdom? I am humbled just knowing that You accept me as Your child. You have not chosen me for who I am or for anything good I have done. I am Yours because of mercy. Thank You for saving me from my pitiful past. I commit the rest of my life to You for use in Your kingdom. *Amen.*

The name of Jesus is the one
lever that lifts the world.

UNKNOWN

The dying Jesus is the evidence of God's
anger toward sin; but the living Jesus is
the proof of God's love and forgiveness.

LORENZ EIFERT

Perfect

Redemption

*But as many as received him, to them
gave he power to become the sons of God,
even to them that believe on his name.*

JOHN 1:12 KJV

*E*ve had it made. A peaceful home, a perfect
relationship with her husband, and an intimate
bond with God. But as soon as the serpent
beguiled her to eat the forbidden fruit,
everything changed. Her disobedience brought
guilt and shame. Suddenly, there was strife in
her marriage, and for the first time ever, she was
afraid of God. The peaceful paradise she had
enjoyed was forever lost, not just to her and
Adam, but to every human being who came
afterward.

Jesus came to restore all that was stolen by
the Deceiver on that fateful day. His sacrifice
broke the curse of sin and made it possible for
us to have a relationship with God once again.

With our guilty stains washed away and our spiritual innocence restored, we can enjoy the same peace that the first humans experienced in Eden.

Christ's redemption is complete and powerful. When hearts are surrendered to Him, wounded relationships, broken marriages, and fragmented homes can all be restored. Though tremors from the first shock of sin are still felt in our fallen world, we can be separated from it. Our mortal bodies are weak, and we are affected by human emotions, yet our hearts can remain morally pure. Not by our own strength or might, but by the awesome power of the cross.

He sent redemption to his people; he has commanded his covenant forever. Holy and awesome is his name!

PSALM 111:9 ESV

But when the right time came, God sent his Son, born of a woman, subject to the law. God sent him to buy freedom for us who were slaves to the law, so that he could adopt us as his very own children.

GALATIANS 4:4–5 NLT

Christ is the Son of God who died for
the redemption of sinners and resurrected
after three days. This is the greatest
truth in the universe.

WATCHMAN NEE

I thought I could have leaped from earth
to heaven at one spring when I first saw
my sins drowned in the Redeemer's blood.

CHARLES H. SPURGEON

At the heart of Christianity there is
a mystery, but it is not the mystery
of intellectual appreciation;
it is the mystery of redemption.

WILLIAM BARCLAY

For the wages of sin is death;
but the gift of God is eternal life
through Jesus Christ our Lord.

ROMANS 6:23 KJV

Yes, Adam's one sin brings condemnation
for everyone, but Christ's one act of
righteousness brings a right relationship
with God and new life for everyone.

ROMANS 5:18 NLT

Prayer of the Broken

Lord, You see my past and the terrible things
I've done. You know the people I've hurt and
those who have hurt me. I am haunted by my
guilt. Deliver me from my wickedness, oh Lord.
Rescue me from the pit that I have dug for
myself. You said that You would not despise a
broken and contrite heart, oh Lord,
so I bring You mine. *Amen.*

Jesus gave his life for our sins, just as
God our Father planned, in order to rescue
us from this evil world in which we live.

GALATIANS 1:4 NLT

God has united you with Christ Jesus. For our benefit God
made him to be wisdom itself. Christ made us right with
God; he made us pure and holy, and he freed us from sin.

1 CORINTHIANS 1:30 NLT

I'm redeemed by thy blood, from the power of
the grave, and the vict'ry I have over death;
Oh, that wonderful flood! Oh, I felt it's pow'r
to save, when I plunged in its fathomless depth!

J. C. FISHER

It is to the Cross that the Christian is
challenged to follow his Master: no path of
redemption can make a detour around it.

HANS URS VON BALTHASAR

The Spirit himself testifies with our spirit that we are God's children.

ROMANS 8:16 NIV

He gave his life to free us from every kind of sin, to cleanse us, and to make us his very own people, totally committed to doing good deeds.

TITUS 2:14 NLT

Let the redeemed of the LORD say so, whom he hath redeemed from the hand of the enemy.

PSALM 107:2 KJV

Restoring

Dear God, You have forgiven my sins, but there are so many other things in my life that need to be fixed. I've made a lot of messes that I can't clean up on my own. Give me wisdom to know what I can repair and what I should leave in Your hands. Help me obey what You have already shown me, and continue to lead me on my journey through this life. *Amen.*

Shall I tell you why I ceased from folly? Why I turned away from sin? 'Twas because the love of my Redeemer fully won my heart to him.

B. E. WARREN

Jesus Christ is the beginning, the middle, and the end of all. In the Gospels he walks in human form upon the earth, and accomplishes the work of redemption.

PHILIP SCHAFF

The atonement in Jesus Christ's blood is perfect; there isn't anything that can be added to it. It is spotless, impeccable, flawless. It is perfect as God is perfect.

A. W. TOZER

The Purchase
of Blood

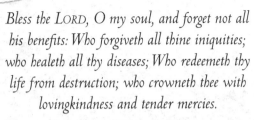

*Bless the LORD, O my soul, and forget not all
his benefits: Who forgiveth all thine iniquities;
who healeth all thy diseases; Who redeemeth thy
life from destruction; who crowneth thee with
lovingkindness and tender mercies.*

PSALM 103:2–5 KJV

We often live beneath our privileges. We learn
to put up with what's wrong in our lives, rather
than asking God to make it right. Instead
of pressing Him for what we need, we get
accustomed to our lack. But Christ didn't shed
His blood so that we could remain defeated.
He purchased everything that our soul craves.
All we have to do is ask Him for it.

Is your soul burdened with the guilt of
sin? Jesus was wounded for our transgressions.
When we repent of our wickedness, His kiss
of forgiveness drives away all condemnation.
Do you find yourself anxious and fretful?

He was chastised for our peace. Is your heart broken by pain and loss? By the Savior's stripes we are healed.

Christ bore our grief and carried our sorrows. He was oppressed and afflicted, endured heavy temptation, was hungry and homeless and despised by the very ones He came to deliver. Even as His flesh recoiled from the horror of the cross, His great love compelled Him to endure it. The blood that dripped from His crowned forehead and spilled from His wounded side is a fountain that still flows today.

There is a Balm in Gilead. It's right at your fingertips. Reach out and touch Him.

For sin shall not have dominion over you:
for ye are not under the law, but under grace.

ROMANS 6:14 KJV

But if we walk in the light, as he is in the light,
we have fellowship one with another, and the blood
of Jesus Christ his Son cleanseth us from all sin.

I JOHN 1:7 KJV

The LORD redeemeth the soul of his servants:
and none of them that trust in him shall be desolate.

PSALM 34:22 KJV

My sin, oh, the bliss of this glorious thought!
My sin, not in part but the whole,
Is nailed to the cross, and I bear it no more,
Praise the Lord, praise the Lord, O my soul!

HORATIO G. SPAFFORD

The Word is a glass to show us
our spots, and Christ's blood is
a fountain to wash them away.

THOMAS WATSON

There is a fountain filled with blood
drawn from Emmanuel's veins;
And sinners plunged beneath that
flood lose all their guilty stains.

WILLIAM COWPER

For by grace you have been saved through faith. And this is not your own doing; it is the gift of God.

EPHESIANS 2:8 ESV

But now in Christ Jesus you who once were far away have been brought near by the blood of Christ.

EPHESIANS 2:13 NIV

For God hath not given us the spirit of fear; but of power, and of love, and of a sound mind.

2 TIMOTHY 1:7 KJV

A Pure Heart

Dear Father, You gave the best that heaven had to offer so that I could be free from my sin and myself. I don't want that sacrifice to be in vain in my life. Create in me a clean heart, oh Lord, and make my spirit pure. Help me to walk in the light of Your Word so that my life can glorify Christ and His sacrifice. *Amen.*

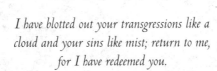

I have blotted out your transgressions like a cloud and your sins like mist; return to me, for I have redeemed you.

Isaiah 44:22 esv

For this is my blood of the covenant, which is poured out for many for the forgiveness of sins.

Matthew 26:28 esv

How much more will the blood of Christ, who through the eternal Spirit offered himself without blemish to God, purify our conscience from dead works to serve the living God.

Hebrews 9:14 esv

We must know the power of the Blood
if we are to know the power of God.

R. A. TORREY

O precious is the flow
That makes me white as snow!
No other fount I know,
Nothing but the blood of Jesus.

ROBERT LOWRY

It costs God nothing, so far as we know,
to create nice things; but to convert
rebellious wills cost Him crucifixion.

C. S. LEWIS

*He personally carried our sins in his
body on the cross so that we can be
dead to sin and live for what is right.
By his wounds you are healed.*

I PETER 2:24 NLT

*In him we have redemption through his
blood, the forgiveness of our trespasses,
according to the riches of his grace.*

EPHESIANS 1:7 ESV

*There is therefore now no condemnation
to them which are in Christ Jesus,
who walk not after the flesh,
but after the Spirit.*

ROMANS 8:1 KJV

Consecration

Lord, without Your grace I am doomed to failure. I can't do what's right in my own strength. I need Your power. You alone can keep me pure and true. You alone can help me endure temptation. I offer my heart as a dwelling place for Your sweet spirit so that You can be with me always and empower me to defeat all that wars against my soul. *Amen.*

God took the worst thing that man could do to his Son, and transformed it into the best thing he could do for man.

UNKNOWN

A chaplain was speaking to a soldier on a cot in a hospital. "You have lost an arm in the great cause," he said. "No," said the soldier with a smile. "I didn't lose it— I gave it." In that same way, Jesus did not lose His life. He gave it purposefully.

UNKNOWN

Mercy's Pardon

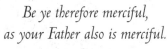

Be ye therefore merciful,
as your Father also is merciful.
LUKE 6:36 KJV

It's not always easy to forgive. Simple misunderstandings can be brushed off, and petty grievances can be reconciled, but some wounds are deep and difficult to heal. Try as we might to forget, painful memories fade slowly. Scenes replay, transporting us back to the moment of injury. We agonize over our own role in the offense, wondering what we might have said or done differently to avoid the whole mess. If left untreated, our hearts can become joyless and miserable, a fertile breeding ground for bitterness and even hatred.

Jesus is our example of forgiveness. He was insulted and slandered, ridiculed by His family members, and betrayed by one of His closest friends. He was beaten and spat upon, falsely accused and condemned to die. Yet even at the height of His agony, Christ said of the jeering crowd, "Father forgive them, they know not what they do." He had mercy on their pitiful human hearts and gave up His right to take vengeance.

Our Savior bids us to walk in His footsteps. His sacrifice reminds us that no matter how grievous the injury, we can find grace to forgive. When we place the injustice—and the one who inflicted it—in God's hands, we begin the healing process. Our hearts do not have to grow brittle with resentment. He who graciously forgave our own trespasses can give us the strength to bestow that same mercy on others.

And be ye kind one to another,
tenderhearted, forgiving one another,
even as God for Christ's sake hath forgiven you.

EPHESIANS 4:32 KJV

The LORD is merciful and gracious,
slow to anger, and plenteous in mercy.

PSALM 103:8 KJV

For I will be merciful toward their iniquities,
and I will remember their sins no more.

HEBREWS 8:12 ESV

I have always found that mercy bears
richer fruits than strict justice.

ABRAHAM LINCOLN

To err is human; to forgive, divine.

ALEXANDER POPE

I believe in the equality of man; and I believe
that religious duties consist in doing justice,
loving mercy, and endeavoring to make our
fellow-creatures happy.

THOMAS PAINE

*The merciful man doeth
good to his own soul. . . .*

PROVERBS 11:17 KJV

*And the LORD passed by before him, and
proclaimed, The LORD, The LORD God,
merciful and gracious, longsuffering, and
abundant in goodness and truth. . . .*

EXODUS 34:6 KJV

*For God has consigned all
to disobedience, that he
may have mercy on all.*

ROMANS 11:32 ESV

Help Me Forgive

Lord, it is not Your will for me to harbor resentment toward those who have wronged me. I want to obey You in all things, and Your Word teaches me to forgive others just as You have forgiven me. Some things are hard to let go of, Lord. For my own soul's sake, help me to place all that troubles me in Your hands and let Your touch heal my wounds. *Amen.*

*For if you forgive other people when they sin against you,
your heavenly Father will also forgive you.*

MATTHEW 6:14 NIV

*The LORD is good to all: and his
tender mercies are over all his works.*

PSALM 145:9 KJV

*Let us fall into the hands of
the LORD, for his mercy is great.*

2 SAMUEL 24:14 NLT

Where mercy, love, and pity dwell,
there God is dwelling too.

WILLIAM BLAKE

Nothing humbles and breaks the
heart of a sinner like mercy and love.

THOMAS BROOKS

The quality of mercy is not strained;
It droppeth as the gentle rain from heaven
Upon the place beneath. It is twice blessed—
It blesseth him that gives, and him that takes.

WILLIAM SHAKESPEARE

Blessed are the merciful,
for they shall receive mercy.

MATTHEW 5:7 ESV

Since God chose you to be the holy
people he loves, you must clothe
yourselves with tenderhearted mercy,
kindness, humility, gentleness, and
patience. Make allowance for each
other's faults, and forgive anyone who
offends you. Remember, the Lord
forgave you, so you must forgive others.

COLOSSIANS 3:12–13 NLT

Behold, we count them happy which
endure. Ye have heard of the patience
of Job, and have seen the end of the
Lord; that the Lord is very pitiful,
and of tender mercy.

JAMES 5:11 KJV

The Big Picture

Dear God, when I think of what Jesus suffered on the cross, it makes the offenses that trouble me seem so petty. And yet, they do trouble me. Show me the big picture, Lord. When I'm tempted to hold a grudge, remind me of the cross. Help me to step over the stumbling blocks placed in my path so that I can press joyfully onward to heaven. *Amen.*

Being all fashioned of the self-same dust,
Let us be merciful as well as just.

HENRY WADSWORTH LONGFELLOW

Teach me to feel another's woe,
To hide the fault I see:
That mercy I to others show,
That mercy show to me.

ALEXANDER POPE

There's a wideness in God's mercy,
Like the wideness of the sea;
There's a kindness in his justice,
Which is more than liberty.

FREDERICK W. FABER

Promises

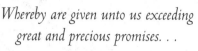

*Whereby are given unto us exceeding
great and precious promises. . .*

2 PETER 1:4 KJV

*M*aking promises is one thing. Keeping them is another. Despite good intentions, human vows are unreliable at best. But heaven and earth will pass away before one of God's words will fail. Our confidence in His promises gives comfort and courage like nothing else can.

An uncertain future isn't as troubling when we remember Jeremiah 29:11. If we're struggling with finances, we have the promise from Philippians 4:19 that God will supply all of our needs. In seasons of temptation, we can lean on 1 Corinthians 10:13 and look for our way of escape. If we lack wisdom, James 1:5 tells us to ask God for it. When it seems that our entire life is crumbling to dust at our feet, we can take courage in knowing, according to

Romans 8:28, that all things work together for our good.

As wonderful as these promises are, nothing gives more hope than the one found in I Corinthians 2:9 (KJV). "Eye hath not seen, nor ear heard, neither have entered into the heart of man, the things which God hath prepared for them that love Him." Eternal life purchased at Calvary for all the redeemed, is the reward for following Christ to the very end. Tuck this jewel of hope away for those seasons of difficulty when it seems your feet can't take another step. Heaven will be worth it all. God promised it.

*For all of God's promises have been fulfilled in Christ
with a resounding "Yes!" And through Christ, our "Amen"
(which means "Yes") ascends to God for his glory.*

2 CORINTHIANS 1:20 NLT

*He that dwelleth in the secret place of the most
High shall abide under the shadow of the Almighty.*

PSALM 91:1 KJV

*For the promise is for you and for your children
and for all who are far off, everyone whom
the Lord our God calls to himself.*

ACTS 2:39 ESV

Every promise in the book is mine.
Every chapter, every verse, every line,
All are blessings of His love divine.
Every promise in the book is mine.

UNKNOWN

Let God's promises shine on your problems.

CORRIE TEN BOOM

All who call on God in true faith,
earnestly from the heart, will certainly
be heard, and will receive what they
have asked and desired.

MARTIN LUTHER

But my God shall supply all your
need according to his riches
in glory by Christ Jesus.

PHILIPPIANS 4:19 KJV

And we know that all things work
together for good to them that love
God, to them who are the called
according to his purpose.

ROMANS 8:28 KJV

No temptation has overtaken you that
is not common to man. God is faithful,
and he will not let you be tempted
beyond your ability, but with the temp-
tation he will also provide the way of
escape, that you may be able to endure it.

I CORINTHIANS 10:13 ESV

Accepting Promises

Lord, sometimes it's hard for me to accept that Your promises are intended for me. I get discouraged when I can't see Your hand working in my life, or things don't work out the way that I prayed they would. When I'm having a hard time claiming Your promises, remind me that Your will is best and help me to "walk by faith and not by sight" (2 Corinthians 5:7 KJV). *Amen.*

Your promises have been thoroughly tested;
that is why I love them so much.

PSALM 119:140 NLT

In hope of eternal life, which God,
that cannot lie, promised before the world began.

TITUS 1:2 KJV

"For I know the plans I have for you," declares
the LORD, "plans to prosper you and not to
harm you, plans to give you hope and a future."

JEREMIAH 29:11 NIV

God's gifts put man's best dreams to shame.

Elizabeth Barrett Browning

God didn't promise days without pain,
laughter without sorrow, sun without rain,
but He did promise strength for the day,
comfort for the tears, and light for the way.

Unknown

No pillow so soft as God's promise.

Unknown

*I am leaving you with a gift—
peace of mind and heart. And the
peace I give is a gift the world cannot
give. So don't be troubled or afraid.*

JOHN 14:27 NLT

*But my God shall supply all your
need according to his riches in
glory by Christ Jesus.*

PHILIPPIANS 4:19 KJV

*God blesses those who patiently endure
testing and temptation. Afterward they
will receive the crown of life that God
has promised to those who love him.*

JAMES 1:12 NLT

*And this is the promise that he hath
promised us, even eternal life.*

I JOHN 2:25 KJV

Promise of Heaven

Dear Lord, this world can be so depressing.
Wars and rumors of wars, crime, disease,
financial collapse. . .sometimes I'm truly afraid
of what the future holds. But Your Word tells
me that this world is not my home. When
I'm feeling apprehensive about things I can't
control, remind me that this life is fleeting.
Help me to keep my chin up and my eyes
on the eternal prize. *Amen.*

All that I have seen teaches me to trust
God for all I have not seen.

UNKNOWN

I know God will not give me anything
I can't handle. I just wish that He
didn't trust me so much.

MOTHER TERESA

Standing on the promises, I cannot fall,
List'ning every moment to the Spirit's call,
Resting in my Savior, as my all in all,
Standing on the promises of God.

R. KELSO CARTER

True Belief

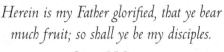

Herein is my Father glorified, that ye bear much fruit; so shall ye be my disciples.

JOHN 15:8 KJV

It's easier to believe than to follow, to read the Bible than obey it, to possess faith than to act on it. But belief without deeds is useless. God gets no glory out of an empty profession. When we call ourselves Christians, our actions should mirror our Master's.

There were plenty of people who believed in Jesus when He walked the shores of Galilee, but few who gave up everything to follow Him. Many were offended by His preaching because He challenged motives as well as deeds. Though compassionate and merciful, He wasn't afraid to proclaim judgment. He commanded repentance and told people to go and sin no more.

In our lukewarm age, it's easy to be a lazy believer. Temptations are strong, and the flesh is weak. When people get on our nerves or traffic is frustrating, we may feel justified in venting a few muttered curses. If telling the truth isn't convenient, we might allow for a little massaging of the facts. But when we choose to disobey God's Word, we give nonbelievers the impression that Christianity is just another powerless religion. When we stand for what's right and refuse to compromise our values, we become a beacon of righteousness that lifts up the One who enables us to do so.

Actions speak louder than words. What do yours say? Are you a true believer?

*If I do not the works of my Father, believe me not.
But if I do, though ye believe not me, believe the
works: that ye may know, and believe, that the
Father is in me, and I in him.*

JOHN 10:37–38 KJV

*For those who are led by the Spirit
of God are the children of God.*

ROMANS 8:14 NIV

If ye love me, keep my commandments.

JOHN 14:15 KJV

To be like Christ is to be a Christian.

WILLIAM PENN

Let your words be the genuine
picture of your heart.

JOHN WESLEY

Confidence on the outside begins by
living with integrity on the inside.

UNKNOWN

*By this shall all men know that
ye are my disciples, if ye
have love one to another.*

JOHN 13:35 KJV

*And we can be sure that we know him
if we obey his commandments. . . .*

1 JOHN 2:3–4 NLT

*Therefore if any man be in Christ, he
is a new creature: old things are passed
away; behold, all things are become new.*

2 CORINTHIANS 5:17 KJV

Cherish the Cross

Dear Father, this world provides plenty of excuses to do the wrong thing, but You have called me to do what's right. Prick my heart if I begin to make excuses for sin. Keep me strong when I am tempted to stray. Christ sacrificed everything to rescue me from the dangerous path I was on. Remind me of what my sin cost Him, and help me to cherish my salvation. *Amen.*

Let's not merely say that we love each other;
let us show the truth by our actions.

1 JOHN 3:18 NLT

Then he said to them all: "Whoever wants to
be my disciple must deny themselves and take
up their cross daily and follow me."

LUKE 9:23 NIV

For I have given you an example,
that ye should do as I have done to you.

JOHN 13:15 KJV

Out of our beliefs are born deeds;
out of our deeds we form habits;
out of our habits grows our character;
and on our character we build our destiny.

HENRY HANCOCK

Lie not, neither to thyself, nor man,
nor God. It is for cowards to lie.

GEORGE HERBERT

Keep true, never be ashamed of doing
right, decide on what you think is
right and stick to it.

GEORGE ELIOT

Not every one that saith unto me, Lord, Lord, shall enter into the kingdom of heaven; but he that doeth the will of my Father which is in heaven.

MATTHEW 7:21 KJV

So in everything, do to others what you would have them do to you, for this sums up the Law and the Prophets.

MATTHEW 7:12 NIV

Then the way you live will always honor and please the Lord, and your lives will produce every kind of good fruit. All the while, you will grow as you learn to know God better and better.

COLOSSIANS 1:10 NLT

Help Me Shine

Lord, when others look at my life, I want them to see Jesus. Let my actions testify what He has done in my heart. Warn me when I become too casual about my faith. Tap me on the shoulder if I get careless. Keep me true to Your Word. Help me to be a beacon of light in this dark world, showing others the way to Christ. *Amen.*

[To have faith in Christ] means, of course, trying to do all that He says. There would be no sense in saying you trusted a person if you would not take his advice.

C. S. LEWIS

There are many of us that are willing to do great things for the Lord, but few of us are willing to do little things.

D. L. MOODY

What good is having someone who can walk on water if you don't follow in his footsteps?

UNKNOWN

Gathering
Wisdom

*All scripture is given by inspiration of God,
and is profitable for doctrine, for reproof, for
correction, for instruction in righteousness.*

2 TIMOTHY 3:16 KJV

Regardless of how the Bible is viewed by an unbelieving world, true Christians understand that it is God's personal message to us. The stories may have taken place thousands of years ago, but the precepts hold true today. Villains and heroes from both testaments teach us valuable lessons about the follies of disobedience and the reward of faithfulness.

God's Word is alive. Though penned centuries ago by faithful writers, His Spirit witnesses to our hearts that what we read is true. When we obey that revealed Word, we grow in grace and wisdom. Just as the Israelites gathered manna each morning in the wilderness, so we should gather the nourishing bread of heaven. Our physical bodies grow weak from lack of food, and the same is true of our souls. Every Christian wants to grow and mature, but it will never happen unless we consistently feed on God's Word.

Taking the time to gather our soul's manna requires effort. The cares of life will rob every minute of our day, if we let them. But when we esteem the Words of God more than our necessary food (Job 23:12), we're willing to do whatever it takes. Have you read the Bible today? If not, take a few minutes to search the scriptures and see what the Lord has especially for you.

I delight in your decrees;
I will not neglect your word.

PSALM 119:16 NIV

This is what the LORD says—your Redeemer,
the Holy One of Israel: "I am the LORD your God,
who teaches you what is best for you, who directs
you in the way you should go."

ISAIAH 48:17 NIV

For the LORD giveth wisdom: out of his
mouth cometh knowledge and understanding.

PROVERBS 2:6 KJV

I prayed for faith, and thought that some-
day, faith would come down and strike
me like lightning. But faith did not seem to
come. One day I read in the tenth chapter
of Romans, "Now faith cometh by hearing,
and hearing by the Word of God." I had
closed my Bible, and prayed for faith. I now
opened my Bible, and began to study,
and faith has been growing ever since.

DWIGHT L. MOODY

To acknowledge you were wrong yesterday
is to acknowledge you are wiser today.

CHARLES H. SPURGEON

Intelligent people are always ready to learn. Their ears are open for knowledge.

PROVERBS 18:15 NLT

If you need wisdom, ask our generous God, and he will give it to you. He will not rebuke you for asking.

JAMES 1:5 NLT

Wisdom is the principal thing; therefore get wisdom: and with all thy getting get understanding.

PROVERBS 4:7 KJV

Overcoming "Later"

Lord, I know You want me to read Your Word, but sometimes I have a hard time doing so. With all of my duties and responsibilities, it's easy to put off Bible reading until later. But then "later" becomes days and even weeks! Forgive me for neglecting the scriptures. Help me to see that reading them is a privilege and a blessing, not just another duty to cross off my list. *Amen.*

*Because the foolishness of God is wiser than men;
and the weakness of God is stronger than men.*

I CORINTHIANS 1:25 KJV

*Show me your ways, LORD, teach me your paths.
Guide me in your truth and teach me, for you are God
my Savior, and my hope is in you all day long.*

PSALM 25:4–5 NIV

*Teach me good judgment and knowledge:
for I have believed thy commandments.*

PSALM 119:66 KJV

I am hardly sure of anything but
what God has revealed to me.

JOHN WESLEY

Seek not to grow in knowledge chiefly
for the sake of applause, and to enable
you to dispute with others; but seek
it for the benefit of your souls.

JONATHAN EDWARDS

If ye keep watch over your hearts,
and listen for the Voice of God and
learn of Him, in one short hour ye can
learn more from Him than ye could learn
from Man in a thousand years.

JOHANNES TAULER

Every word of God proves true.
He is a shield to all who come
to him for protection.
PROVERBS 30:5 NLT

The fear of the LORD is the beginning of
wisdom: a good understanding have all
they that do his commandments:
his praise endureth for ever.
PSALM 111:10 KJV

For the LORD corrects those he loves,
just as a father corrects a child
in whom he delights.
PROVERBS 3:12 NLT

Bread of Heaven

Dear God, thank You for Your Word. It truly is
a lamp unto my feet and a light unto my path.
You know what I need today. Guide me as I
read the scriptures, and lead me to the answers I
am seeking. Feed me with the bread of heaven,
and help me to hide it deep in my heart,
so I can access it in the time of need. *Amen.*

The end of all learning is to know God, and
out of that knowledge to love and imitate Him.

JOHN MILTON

Learning is not attained by chance,
it must be sought for with ardor
and attended to with diligence.

ABIGAIL ADAMS

Wisdom is the right use of knowledge.
To know is not to be wise. Many men know
a great deal, and are all the greater fools
for it. There is no fool so great a fool as
a knowing fool. But to know how to use
knowledge is to have wisdom.

CHARLES H. SPURGEON

His Still,
Small Voice

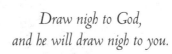

Draw nigh to God,
and he will draw nigh to you.
JAMES 4:8 KJV

*W*e love to hear God's voice. His kind,
affirming words lend boldness and confidence.
No enemy is too fierce and no circumstance
too great. But when we cease to hear from
Him, we become fretful and troubled. Even
His chastisement is preferred over silence,
because reproof assures us that we are indeed
His children. Our heart craves communion
with the Lord. When it's lacking, we feel it to
the depths of our soul.

Even when we cannot sense God's presence,
faith assures us that He is near. But sometimes
His distance is a result of our own carelessness.
Our daily journeys to the throne of grace
are sometimes postponed while we attend to
louder demands. If those delays become habit,

we may eventually find ourselves neglecting prayer altogether.

In order to hear God's still, small voice, we must draw as near to Him as possible. Prayer cannot be reserved for times of crisis and need. We must meet with our heavenly Father daily, even if we can't make it to our secret prayer closet. God isn't picky about time or place. He'll listen to us when we're up to our elbows in dishwater, in the rocking chair with a fussy baby, or driving down the highway.

Nothing is sweeter to the soul than hearing God's voice, and nothing thrills Him more than hearing from you. Have you been to His throne today?

*And he said, Go forth, and stand upon the mount
before the L*ORD*. And, behold, the L*ORD *passed by,
and a great and strong wind rent the mountains,
and brake in pieces the rocks before the L*ORD*; but the
L*ORD *was not in the wind: and after the wind an
earthquake; but the L*ORD *was not in the earthquake:
And after the earthquake a fire; but the L*ORD *was
not in the fire: and after the fire a still small voice.*

I KINGS 19:11–12 KJV

Be still, and know that I am God.

PSALM 46:10 KJV

Don't pray when you feel like it. Have an appointment with the Lord and keep it. A man is powerful on his knees.

CORRIE TEN BOOM

When God speaks he speaks so loudly that all the voices of the world seem dumb. And yet when God speaks he speaks so softly that no one hears the whisper but yourself.

HENRY DRUMMOND

God understands our prayers even when we can't find the words to say them.

UNKNOWN

*But when you pray, go away by
yourself, shut the door behind you,
and pray to your Father in private.
Then your Father, who sees
everything, will reward you.*

MATTHEW 6:6 NLT

*Likewise the Spirit helps us in our
weakness. For we do not know what
to pray for as we ought, but the Spirit
himself intercedes for us with
groanings too deep for words.*

ROMANS 8:26 ESV

*Seek the LORD and his strength,
seek his face continually.*

I CHRONICLES 16:11 KJV

Managing Priorities

Lord, my soul craves to spend time alone with You, even though my flesh doesn't. There are so many things to distract me from Your throne of grace. Some of them aren't even important! Show me how to organize my schedule so that I am using my time wisely instead of wasting it on frivolous things. Help me to keep my priorities in order, making sure that You stay in first place. *Amen.*

*And without faith it is impossible to please God, because
anyone who comes to him must believe that he exists
and that he rewards those who earnestly seek him.*

HEBREWS 11:6 NIV

*Ask, and it shall be given you; seek, and ye shall find;
knock, and it shall be opened unto you: For every
one that asketh receiveth; and he that seeketh findeth;
and to him that knocketh it shall be opened.*

MATTHEW 7:7–8 KJV

Certain thoughts are prayers. There are
moments when, whatever be the attitude
of the body, the soul is on its knees.

VICTOR HUGO

He who kneels before God
can stand before anyone.

UNKNOWN

You may as soon find a living man
that does not breathe, as a living
Christian that does not pray.

MATTHEW HENRY

Unto thee will I cry, O LORD
my rock; be not silent to me.
PSALM 28:1 KJV

Be careful for nothing; but in every
thing by prayer and supplication
with thanksgiving let your requests
be made known unto God.
PHILIPPIANS 4:6 KJV

Hear me, LORD, my plea is just;
listen to my cry. Hear my prayer—
it does not rise from deceitful lips.
PSALM 17:1 NIV

Pray without ceasing.
I THESSALONIANS 5:17 KJV

Pray On

Lord, I need answers that only You can provide, and they don't always come when I'd like them to. Deep down inside, I know that You're listening, but sometimes it's easy to doubt. Be not silent to me, Oh Lord. Answer Your servant when I cry. And no matter how alone I may feel when I bow before Your throne, help me to keep praying until the answer comes. *Amen.*

Those persons who know the deep peace
of God, the unfathomable peace that
passeth all understanding, are always
men and women of much prayer.

R. A. TORREY

Groanings which cannot be uttered are
often prayers which cannot be refused.

CHARLES H. SPURGEON

Softly I hear him calling,
calling at close of day;
Sweetly his tones are falling,
"Come to the throne and pray."

CLARA M. BROOKS

Rejoicing
in Jesus

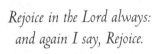

Rejoice in the Lord always:
and again I say, Rejoice.
PHILIPPIANS 4:4 KJV

*J*oyful Christians are strong Christians. That's why our adversary works so hard to discourage us. Nothing takes the fight out of a child of God like a good dose of depression. And there's plenty in this world to be depressed about. But though we face tribulations in this life, Jesus told us to be of good cheer. He overcame the world, and through His grace and power, we can, too.

Joy doesn't come from what we own, or how we feel. All of those things are fleeting. But the joy of the Lord runs deep, springing from a divine well that can't be stopped up by earthly woes. It puts a smile on our face when we have reason to scowl. It picks us up when life lays us flat. It turns our complaints into praises and our tears into laughter. Even in times of deepest despair, we find the strength to keep calm and carry on.

Heaven-bound souls can't linger in the dumps for long, and if you find yourself there, it's time to take action. Boot out those joy robbers with praise. Put on some worship music, and make a joyful noise unto the Lord. Sing a hymn, if only to yourself. Recount your blessings, naming each one to God in prayer. Most of all, keep your eyes on Jesus. The only way to overcome the world's sorrows is to stay focused on Him.

*This is the day which the L*ORD *hath made;*
we will rejoice and be glad in it.

PSALM 118:24 KJV

May the God of hope fill you with all joy and
peace in believing, so that by the power of the
Holy Spirit you may abound in hope.

ROMANS 15:13 ESV

That your rejoicing may be more
abundant in Jesus Christ. . .

PHILIPPIANS 1:26 KJV

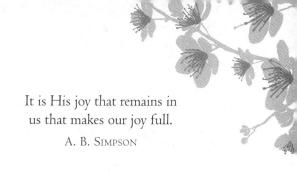

It is His joy that remains in
us that makes our joy full.

A. B. SIMPSON

When was the last time you laughed for the
sheer joy of your salvation? People are not
attracted to somber doctrines. There is no
persuasive power in a gloomy and morbid
religion. Let the world see your joy, and you
won't be able to keep them away. To be
filled with God is to be filled with joy.

UNKNOWN

The life of a true Christian should
be a perpetual jubilee, a prelude
to the festivals of eternity.

THEOPHANE VENARD

I will greatly rejoice in the LORD,
my soul shall be joyful in my God;
for he hath clothed me with the garments
of salvation, he hath covered me with
the robe of righteousness. . . .
ISAIAH 61:10 KJV

Then my soul will rejoice in the
LORD and delight in his salvation.
PSALM 35:9 NIV

Yet I will rejoice in the LORD,
I will joy in the God of my salvation.
HABAKKUK 3:18 KJV

Midnight Praises

Lord, there are some days when rejoicing is the last thing on my mind. I know I'm not the only one who's been there. If You gave Paul and Silas the grace to sing praises in their prison cell at midnight, You can give me the grace to overcome my dismal times. Help me to keep things in perspective, rather than allowing my trials to get the best of me. *Amen.*

And the ransomed of the LORD shall return and
come to Zion with singing; everlasting joy shall be
upon their heads; they shall obtain gladness and joy,
and sorrow and sighing shall flee away.

ISAIAH 35:10 ESV

You love him even though you have never seen him.
Though you do not see him now, you trust him;
and you rejoice with a glorious, inexpressible joy.

I PETER 1:8 NLT

Happiness is caused by things that happen around me, and circumstances will mar it; but joy flows right on through trouble; joy flows on through the dark; joy flows in the night as well as in the day; joy flows all through persecution and opposition.

D. L. MOODY

Joy is the serious business of Heaven.

C. S. LEWIS

Happiness depends on happenings;
joy depends on Christ.

UNKNOWN

*Don't be dejected and sad, for the joy
of the LORD is your strength!*

NEHEMIAH 8:10 NLT

*Clap your hands, all you nations;
shout to God with cries of joy.*

PSALM 47:1 NIV

*But let all those that put their trust in
thee rejoice: let them ever shout for joy,
because thou defendest them: let them also
that love thy name be joyful in thee.*

PSALM 5:11 KJV

150

Ambassador of Joy

Dear Father, help me to shower joy on others. There are so many hurting people around me who could use a kind word. Remind me that rudeness often masks a broken heart. Season my speech with grace, and help me to be gentle and sweet, no matter who I am dealing with. I want my actions to draw others toward You so that they can know the joy that I have. *Amen.*

The joy of the Lord will arm us against the assaults of our spiritual enemies and put our mouths out of taste for those pleasures with which the tempter baits his hooks.

MATTHEW HENRY

If you have no joy, there's a leak in your Christianity somewhere.

BILLY SUNDAY

No one can get Joy by merely asking for it. It is one of the ripest fruits of the Christian life, and, like all fruits, must be grown.

HENRY DRUMMOND

Gathering for

Praise

Enter into his gates with thanksgiving,
and into his courts with praise: be thankful
unto him, and bless his name.

PSALM 100:4 KJV

We can meet with the Lord anywhere and at any time, but worshipping Him alone on a mountaintop doesn't encourage others or enlighten ourselves. God wants all of His people to worship together in unity and fellowship. It doesn't much matter where that meeting takes place. As long as two or three are gathered in Jesus' name, He's there, too (Matthew 18:20).

Church is a place of praise. God isn't glorified when we attend services out of habit or duty, then sit in our pew like the proverbial bump on a log. His Word tells us to teach and admonish one another "in psalms and hymns and spiritual songs, singing with grace in your hearts to the Lord" (Colossians 3:16 KJV).

Like everyone else, Christians get weary and discouraged. But when we belong to God's great family, we never have to weep alone. Church is a place to share our burdens, pray for them together, and rejoice as one when the answer finally comes.

If you don't have a church home, you're missing out on something special. Finding one can seem overwhelming, but when we ask God to lead us to the right body of believers, He will be faithful to do so. Take time for church this Sunday. You might be surprised at what the Lord has in store there for you.

*One thing have I desired of the L{\small ORD}, that will
I seek after; that I may dwell in the house of the
L{\small ORD} all the days of my life, to behold the beauty
of the L{\small ORD}, and to enquire in his temple.*

P{\small SALM} 27:4 {\small KJV}

*Then I will thank you in front of the great assembly.
I will praise you before all the people.*

P{\small SALM} 35:18 {\small NLT}

When large numbers of people share
their joy in common, the happiness
of each is greater because each
adds fuel to the other's flame.

St Augustine

Church attendance is as vital to a
disciple as a transfusion of rich,
healthy blood to a sick man.

Dwight L. Moody

Praise, now, is one of the great
duties of the redeemed.

Albert Barnes

Let us think of ways to motivate one another to acts of love and good works. And let us not neglect our meeting together, as some people do, but encourage one another, especially now that the day of his return is drawing near.

HEBREWS 10:24–25 NLT

I was glad when they said unto me, Let us go into the house of the LORD.

PSALM 122:1 KJV

Pressing Out

Dear God, I don't always feel like going to church. Sometimes I'd rather sleep in on Sunday mornings, or catch up on things that I can't get to during the week. But worshipping You is more important than any of the things that distract me from Your service. Help me to press my way to Your House no matter how I feel. *Amen.*

Those that be planted in the house of the
LORD shall flourish in the courts of our God.

PSALM 92:13 KJV

I will declare thy name unto my brethren:
in the midst of the congregation will I praise thee.

PSALM 22:22 KJV

With my mouth I will greatly extol the LORD;
in the great throng of worshipers I will praise him.

PSALM 109:30 NIV

When a Christian shuns fellowship
with other Christians, the devil smiles.

CORRIE TEN BOOM

It is one thing for the living water to
descend from Christ into the heart,
and another thing how—when it has
descended—it moves the heart to
worship. All power of worship in the soul,
is the result of the waters flowing into it,
and their flowing back again to God.

G. V. WIGRAM

Without worship, we go about miserable.

A. W. TOZER

*Praise the LORD! Sing to the
LORD a new song, his praise
in the assembly of the godly!*

PSALM 149:1 ESV

*Happy are those who hear the joyful
call to worship, for they will walk
in the light of your presence, LORD.*

PSALM 89:15 NLT

*Praise the LORD! I will give thanks
to the LORD with my whole heart,
in the company of the upright,
in the congregation.*

PSALM 111:1 ESV

Seeking

Lord, I need to be in church, but I'm not sure where to go. There are so many denominations, and I don't know which one is right. I believe that You have a church for me somewhere. Please guide me to that place. Lead me to a congregation where my soul can be fed and encouraged so that I can grow spiritually and be all that You want me to be. *Amen.*

Take heed of driving so hard after this world,
as to hinder thyself and family from those
duties towards God, which thou art by grace
obliged to; as private prayer, reading the
scriptures, and Christian conference.

JOHN BUNYAN

Once again we come to the house
of God to unite in songs of praise;
To extol with joy our Redeemer's name
and to tell his works and ways.

CHARLES W. NAYLOR

Cast Your Crown

But God forbid that I should glory,
save in the cross of our Lord Jesus Christ. . . .

GALATIANS 6:14 KJV

The crown is a symbol of victory. Kings of old didn't get to wear them unless first there had been bloodshed. Ancient powers were always struggling to reign over each other, and when one finally conquered, he earned the right to wear the crown.

Jesus is our conqueror. He triumphed over the forces of evil, winning eternal life for every soul that comes to Him in repentance. And when His shed blood pours over our sinful heart, washing it clean, we receive that crown of life. It is the first of many victories won for us by our Savior, the first of many crowns.

When we are risen from the mire of our sinful past to walk in newness of life, old things are passed away. We begin to reap the blessings of home and family. Others may be influenced by our example and drawn to Christ. God may bestow us with talents and abilities, perhaps even a position of leadership at church.

As we glory in the abundance of our redeemed life, remember who deserves the crown. As soon as it is placed on our head, let us kneel before the Savior and cast it at His feet. Without Him we are nothing. Each victory won, each grace we exhibit, each and every blessing in life, is given to us through the blood of the Lamb.

He alone is worthy.

*The four and twenty elders fall down before him
that sat on the throne, and worship him that liveth
for ever and ever, and cast their crowns before the throne,
saying, Thou art worthy, O Lord, to receive glory
and honour and power. . . .*

REVELATION 4:10–11 KJV

*And when the chief Shepherd shall appear,
ye shall receive a crown of glory that fadeth not away.*

I PETER 5:4 KJV

*Therefore I glory in Christ Jesus
in my service to God.*

ROMANS 15:17 NIV

God created the world out of nothing,
and so long as we are nothing,
He can make something out of us.

MARTIN LUTHER

Be not proud of race, face, place or grace.

CHARLES H. SPURGEON

Moses spent forty years in the king's
palace thinking that he was somebody;
then he lived forty years in the wilderness
finding out that without God he was a
nobody; finally he spent forty more years
discovering how a nobody with God
can be a somebody.

DWIGHT L. MOODY

We also boast in God through our Lord Jesus Christ, through whom we have now received reconciliation.

ROMANS 5:11 NIV

Know ye not that the unrighteous shall not inherit the kingdom of God? . . . And such were some of you: but ye are washed, but ye are sanctified, but ye are justified in the name of the Lord Jesus, and by the Spirit of our God.

I CORINTHIANS 6:9–11 KJV

Therefore, as the Scriptures say, "If you want to boast, boast only about the LORD."

I CORINTHIANS 1:31 NLT

A Humble Plea

Dear Father, I don't want to take any glory that isn't mine. Until You rescued me, my life was meaningless. All that I am and ever hope to be, I owe to You. Keep me humble, Lord. If I start to get puffed up with pride over my accomplishments in life, remind me of the pitiful condition You found me in and how much You saved me from. *Amen.*

*Therefore being justified by faith, we have peace with
God through our Lord Jesus Christ: By whom also
we have access by faith into this grace wherein we stand,
and rejoice in hope of the glory of God.*

ROMANS 5:1–2 KJV

*But let him that glorieth glory in this, that he understandeth
and knoweth me, that I am the LORD which exercise
lovingkindness, judgment, and righteousness, in the earth:
for in these things I delight, saith the LORD.*

JEREMIAH 9:24 KJV

Christ alone is necessary. Apart from Him
we are completely wretched; without Him
we cannot live and dare not die.

A. W. TOZER

God created the world out of nothing,
and so long as we are nothing,
He can make something out of us.

MARTIN LUTHER

Strength, rest, guidance, grace,
help, sympathy, love—all from
God to us! What a list of blessings!

E. STENBOCK

Now there is in store for me the crown of righteousness, which the Lord, the righteous Judge, will award to me on that day—and not only to me, but also to all who have longed for his appearing.

2 TIMOTHY 4:8 NIV

I have been crucified with Christ. It is no longer I who live, but Christ who lives in me. And the life I now live in the flesh I live by faith in the Son of God, who loved me and gave himself for me.

GALATIANS 2:20 ESV

Compassion, Not Contempt

Lord, when I see the way some people live, I feel contempt rising within me. But rather than looking down on the lost, help me to remember what You delivered me from. I could be in their shoes if it hadn't been for Your mercy. Give me a heart of compassion, and help me to reach out to those people. Remind me that any goodness I have comes from You. *Amen.*

The meek man is not a human mouse afflicted with a sense of his own inferiority. He has accepted God's estimate of his own life: In himself, nothing; In God, everything.

A. W. Tozer

He who sides with God cannot fail to win in every encounter; and, whether the result shall be joy or sorrow, failure or success, death or life, we may, under all circumstances, join in the Apostle's shout of victory, "Thanks be unto God which always causeth us to triumph in Christ!"

Hannah Whitall Smith

Glorious

Whatsoever ye do,
do all to the glory of God.
1 Corinthians 10:31 kjv

More beautiful than snow-peaked mountains
and glowing sunsets, more amazing than
the intricate workings of the human body,
more wonderful than anything our minds can
imagine is God's power to change lives. When
broken marriages are healed and restored; when
wounded hearts forgive and goodness repays
evil; when the vilest sinner is transformed into
a child of heaven, then is God truly glorified.

There are no words sufficient to describe
salvation, but we know when it has taken place.
Changed hearts are revealed by changed actions.
The cursing tongue brings forth blessings. The
lustful heart becomes chaste. Selfish souls put
others first, and liars are freed to tell the truth.

God is glorified when His light shines

through us, not only in times of calamity or great sorrow but also in simple everyday life. We don't have to preach the gospel in distant lands or minister to the sick and dying in order to shine for Christ. We need only to obey the Word of the Lord. When we follow Christ's example in our home and community, we testify of the power of the cross. Because without it, we can't love our neighbor or endure injustice. We can't manifest the fruits of the spirit or remain steadfast in times of temptation. But we can do all these things and more through Christ, who strengthens us.

Such is the power of our great Redeemer, and it is glorious.

Let your light so shine before men,
that they may see your good works,
and glorify your Father which is in heaven.

MATTHEW 5:16 KJV

For ye are bought with a price: therefore glorify God in
your body, and in your spirit, which are God's.

I CORINTHIANS 6:20 KJV

The glory of Christianity is
to conquer by forgiveness.

WILLIAM BLAKE

When God makes His presence felt
through us, we are like the burning bush:
Moses never took any heed what
sort of bush it was—he only saw the
brightness of the Lord.

GEORGE ELIOT

Endurance is not just the ability to bear a
hard thing, but to turn it into glory.

WILLIAM BARCLAY

God has given each of you a gift from his great variety of spiritual gifts. Use them well to serve one another. Do you have the gift of speaking? Then speak as though God himself were speaking through you. Do you have the gift of helping others? Do it with all the strength and energy that God supplies. Then everything you do will bring glory to God through Jesus Christ. All glory and power to him forever and ever! Amen.

1 PETER 4:10–11 NLT

As a result of your ministry, they will give glory to God. . . .

2 CORINTHIANS 9:13 NLT

Shine in Me

Lord, I want to mirror the actions of Jesus in everything I do. Sometimes it seems impossible, when I think of my shortcomings and weaknesses. But I don't have to go in my own strength. Your Word tells me that I can do all things through Christ, who makes me strong. Help me to claim that promise so I can let Your glory shine in me. *Amen.*

Sing, O heavens, for the LORD has done this wondrous thing. Shout for joy, O depths of the earth! Break into song, O mountains and forests and every tree! For the LORD has redeemed Jacob and is glorified in Israel.

ISAIAH 44:23 NLT

If you are insulted for the name of Christ, you are blessed, because the Spirit of glory and of God rests upon you.

I PETER 4:14 ESV

He who is completely sanctified,
or cleansed from all sin, and dies
in this state, is fit for glory.

ADAM CLARKE

How quickly passes away
the glory of this world.

THOMAS À KEMPIS

Grace is but glory begun,
and glory is but grace perfected.

JONATHAN EDWARDS

*Whatever you do, work at it with
all your heart, as working for
the Lord, not for human masters.*

COLOSSIANS 3:23 NIV

*Having your conversation honest among
the Gentiles: that, whereas they speak
against you as evildoers, they may by
your good works, which they shall behold,
glorify God in the day of visitation.*

I PETER 2:12 KJV

The Greatest Thing

Lord, there is so much that I want to accomplish
in this life. You know all of my aspirations
and what it will take for me to fulfill them.
But as I strive to realize my dreams, remind
me that the greatest thing I can ever accomplish
is Your will. Order my steps and help me to
walk according to Your purpose each and
every day of my life. *Amen.*

We should always look upon ourselves as
God's servants, placed in God's world,
to do his work; and accordingly labour
faithfully for him; not with a design to
grow rich and great, but to glorify God,
and do all the good we possibly can.

DAVID BRAINERD

I am so wondrously saved from sin,
Jesus so sweetly abides within,
There at the cross where He took me in;
Glory to his name!

ELISHA HOFFMAN

When God makes His presence felt
through us, we are like the burning bush:
Moses never took any heed what
sort of bush it was—he only saw
the brightness of the Lord.

GEORGE ELIOT

Endurance is not just the ability to bear
a hard thing, but to turn it into glory.

WILLIAM BARCLAY

The glory of Christianity is
to conquer by forgiveness.

WILLIAM BLAKE

*Sing, O heavens, for the LORD has done
this wondrous thing. Shout for joy,
O depths of the earth! Break into
song, O mountains and forests and
every tree! For the LORD has redeemed
Jacob and is glorified in Israel.*

ISAIAH 44:23 NLT

*If you are insulted for the name of
Christ, you are blessed, because the Spirit
of glory and of God rests upon you.*

I PETER 4:14 ESV

Glorified by Obedience

Dear Father, I want others to see by my actions the work You have done in my heart. Grant me a tender conscience and help me to respond quickly to the urgings of Your spirit. Challenge me if I become content with anything less than Your perfect will. I know that when I walk in perfect obedience to Your Word, You are glorified in my life. *Amen.*

Having your conversation honest among the Gentiles:
that, whereas they speak against you as evildoers,
they may by your good works, which they shall behold,
glorify God in the day of visitation.

I Peter 2:12 kjv

Whatever you do, work at it with all your heart,
as working for the Lord, not for human masters.

Colossians 3:23 niv